9.95

M

Mountains

by Anna O'Mara

Bridgestone Books

an Imprint of Capstone Press

Facts about Mountains

- Mountains are the highest places on earth.
- When mountains stand together, they form a range.
- The highest mountain in the world is Mount Everest.
- The highest mountain in North America is Mount McKinley in Alaska.

Bridgestone Books are published by Capstone Press • 818 North Willow Street, Mankato, Minnesota 56001
Copyright © 1996 by Capstone Press • All rights reserved • Printed in the United States of America

Library of Congress Cataloging-in-Publication Data
O'Mara, Anna.
    Mountains/Anna O'Mara.
    p. cm.
    Includes bibliographical references and index.
    Summary: Provides basic scientific information about mountains including their height as well as the difference between being folded, faulted, volcanic, and dome.
    ISBN 1-56065-337-X
    1. Mountains--Juvenile literature. [1. Mountains.] I. Title.
GB512.O43 1996
551.4'32--dc20

95-47650
CIP
AC

Photo credits
Jean S. Buldain: cover. FPG International: 4. Scenics, ETC.: 10, 16. Irene Owsley Spector: 8. J.P. Rowan: 12-14, 18-20.

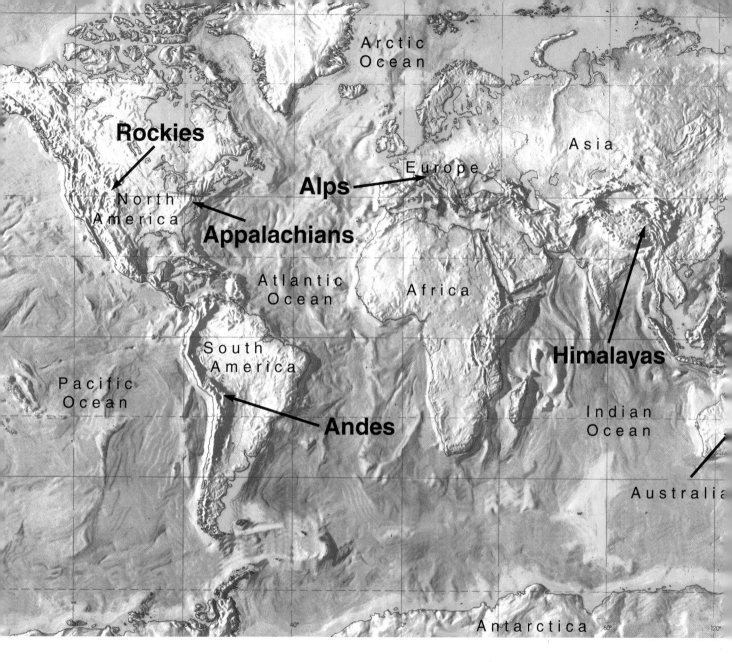

Rockies

Alps

Appalachians

Himalayas

Andes

Arctic
Ocean

Asia

Europe

North
America

Atlantic
Ocean

Africa

Pacific
Ocean

South
America

Indian
Ocean

Australia

Antarctica

Mountain Ranges of the World

Tall Mountains

Mountains stand higher than the land around them. They are larger than hills. Their tops are the highest places on earth.

Some mountains rise 2,000 feet (600 meters) above sea level. Other mountains are much higher.

Mount Everest is the tallest mountain in the world. It is on the border of Tibet and Nepal. It is 29,028 feet (8,708 meters) tall. That is nearly five and a half miles (almost nine kilometers) high. Clouds cover the top of Mount Everest.

The tallest mountain in North America is Mount McKinley. It is in Alaska. It is 20,320 feet (6,096 meters) high. Mount McKinley is also called by its Indian name, Denali. It means the Great One or the High One.

Mount Everest is the tallest mountain in the world.

Table of Contents

Words in **boldface** type in the text are defined in the Words to Know section in the back of this book.

Mountain Ranges

Some mountains stand alone. Mount Fuji in Japan, for example, stands alone. Some mountains stand with other mountains. They form a range.

The Himalayan mountain range is in central Asia. The highest mountains in the world are there. Mount Everest is part of this range.

There are two important ranges in North America. They are the Rocky Mountains and the Appalachian Mountains.

The Rocky Mountains are in the west. They reach from New Mexico to Alaska. The Appalachian range is in the east. These mountains are worn away and rounded.

There is a long range in South America. It is the Andes range. There is a lake on top of this range.

There is a well-known range in Europe. It is the Alps. A long tunnel through the Alps connects France and Italy.

Folded Mountains

Some mountains are folded mountains. They are created when the earth's surface folds.

The surface of the earth is not solid. This crust is made up of rocky pieces called plates. They push and pull against each other.

Sometimes plates move toward each other. After millions of years, the plates bump against each other. When they bump, the earth's crust folds like a piece of cloth. The tops of the rocky folds stick up high above land. They are mountains.

The Himalayas, the Rocky Mountains, the Appalachians, the Andes, and the Alps are folded mountains.

Aspen is a popular ski resort in the Rocky Mountains.

Faulted Mountains

Some mountains are faulted mountains. They are created when the earth's surface opens up.

The rocky pieces of the earth's crust sometimes pull away from one another. The weak places where the rocks break apart are **faults**.

When the rocks break or pull away from one another, they form large blocks. Some of these blocks fall down. Some blocks tip up. Others move sideways. These blocks create faulted mountains.

The Grand Tetons in Wyoming and the Sierra Nevada mountains in California are faulted mountains.

The Sierra Nevada mountains in California are faulted mountains.

Volcanic Mountains and Dome Mountains

Some mountains are volcanic mountains. Hot and melted rock is called **magma**. It moves beneath the earth's crust. Sometimes magma bubbles up between cracks in the crust.

The magma pushes up. It spits **ash** into the sky. The air cools the magma into **lava**. It cools the ash into **tuff.** The lava and the tuff form a mound around the opening in the earth. The mound rises higher and higher. A cone-shaped mountain forms. Mount Vesuvius in Italy and Mount Rainier in Washington are volcanic mountains.

Some mountains are dome mountains. Magma sometimes pushes the earth's crust into a bump. The magma hardens and becomes solid rock again. When this happens, dome mountains are made.

The Black Hills of South Dakota and Wyoming and the Adirondack Mountains of New York are dome mountains.

Poa's Volcano National Park is in Costa Rica.

Mountain Plants

Mountains are so tall that they have many areas of life on them. Different plants grow in each area.

Plants at the bottom are the same as those that grow on the land surrounding the mountain. In this low area, oak and maple trees often grow.

Higher up on the mountain, the air is cooler. Plants and trees do not grow as tall there as at the bottom of a mountain. Pine and spruce forests grow best there.

Near the top of the mountain is the timberline. Because of the cold, trees do not grow higher than the timberline. Only small shrubs and mosses grow above the timberline.

Nothing grows on the tops of the tallest mountains. It is very cold there. Only snow and ice are found on the mountain tops. Some mountain tops have snow all year long.

Fiordland National Park is in the Southern Alps in New Zealand.

Mountain Animals

Many kinds of animals live on mountains. They are suited to the different mountain areas.

Food for the animals is plentiful in the foothills. Foothills are small hills at the bottom of a mountain. Many animals live in this area.

Pine forests grow higher up. Animals there can live on the seeds of pine cones.

Still higher, mountain goats climb the rocky slopes. Thick fur covers their bodies. It protects them from the cold winds.

Snow leopards, pandas, and yaks live high in the Himalayas of Asia. Llamas, alpacas, and vicunas live high in the Andes of South America. Mountain lions and grizzly bears live high in the Rockies of North America.

There are pronghorn living in the Rocky Mountain foothills at Yellowstone National Park.

Mountain People

Mountain air has less oxygen in it than the air at lower levels. People who live high in the mountains breathe this thin air without any problems. They are used to life in the mountains.

Some people who live in the mountains herd animals. In the summer, they lead their sheep and goats up to green pastures. When winter comes, they bring their animals down to the valleys. There they feed the animals hay they have grown.

In China and Southeast Asia, people farm on the steep mountain slopes. Their small fields are called terraces. They look like giant steps up the mountainside.

People in Ecuador live high in the Andes Mountains.

Mountain Erosion

Ice, rain, wind, rushing water, heat, and cold attack mountains. They wear them away. These forces of **erosion** change the shape of mountains.

Rain and melted snow rush down the mountainside. As the water comes down the mountain, it picks up loose rocks. The rocks hit against the sides of the mountain and chip off more rocks. This process is called erosion.

Sometimes a mountain is very tall. The snow and ice on its top do not melt. The ice becomes a **glacier**. The glacier moves slowly down the mountain.

As the glacier moves, it picks up sharp rocks. The rocks and the hard ice rub against the sides of the mountain. They carve out valleys. The mountain becomes rounder and smoother. This is erosion, too.

The Bridalveil Fall is in Yosemite National Park in California.

Hands On: Make an Erupting Volcano

Imagine a mountain **erupting**, or blowing its top. You can make your own model of a volcano and see it happen.

You will need

- plastic soda bottle
- large pan
- small bowl or cup
- 1 tablespoon (15 milliliters) of flour
- 1 tablespoon (15 milliliters) of baking soda
- 1 cup (250 milliliters) of white vinegar
- clay or dirt
- red food coloring
- funnel

How to do it

1. Put the soda bottle in the pan.

2. Put clay or dirt around the bottle to make it look like a cone-shaped mountain. The top of the bottle should stick out of the top of the mountain.

3. Mix the flour and baking soda together. Use the funnel to pour the mixture into the bottle.

4. Put 20 drops of red food coloring in the bottle.

5. Pour about half the vinegar into the bottle. When the foaming stops, add the rest of the vinegar.

Words to Know

ash—fine drops of magma blown out of a volcano

erosion—wearing away land

erupt—to shoot out

faults—breaks in layers of rock

glacier—slow moving river of ice

lava—cooled and hardened magma

magma—hot, liquid rock beneath the earth's crust

tuff—cooled and hardened ash from a volcano

Read More

Curtis, Neil and Michael Allaby. *Planet Earth.* New York: Kingfisher Books, 1993.

Simon, Seymour. *Mountains.* New York: Morrow Junior Books, 1994.

Stone, L.M. *Mountains.* A New True Book. Chicago: Childrens Press, 1983.

Vrbova, Zuza. *Mountains.* Mahwah, N.J.: Troll Associates, 1990.

Useful Addresses

Alpine Club of Canada
Box 2040
Caumore, AB T0L 0C0
Canada

International Mountain Society
Box 1978
Davis, CA 95617-1978

Hawaii Volcanoes National Park
Kilauea Visitor Center
Hawaii National Park, HI 96718

Woodlands Mountain Institute
Box 907
Franklin, WV 26807

Index